1 TIMOTHY
Leading by Example

Scott Hotaling

A DIVISION OF SCRIPTURE PRESS PUBLICATIONS INC.
USA   CANADA   ENGLAND

The Scripture quotations contained herein are from the *New Revised Standard Version of the Bible* (NRSV), © 1989 by the Division of Christian Education of the National Council of the Churches of Christ in the United States of America. All rights reserved.

Editor: Carolyn Nystrom
Designer: Scott Rattray
Cover Photo: Tony Stone Images

Recommended Dewey Decimal Classification: 227.83
Suggested Subject Heading: BIBLE STUDY: 1 TIMOTHY
ISBN: 1-56476-328-5

1 2 3 4 5 6 7 8 9 10 Printing / Year 99 98 97 96 95

Contents

Welcome to TruthSeed

I am a planter. Each spring finds me stooped in my garden, loose dirt churned soft by winter storms oozing into my worn sneakers, the smell of compost twitching my nose, warm sun thawing the muscles of my back, and precious seed—radish, carrots, lettuce, peas, beans, corn, beets, watermelon, cantaloupe, squash, cosmos, marigold, zinnia—trickling through my fingers. It's my favorite phase of gardening, one I try to remember as I tug at thick weeds in late June's humidity, swat mosquitoes in sweltering July twilight, and heft baskets of produce into my August-cluttered kitchen. I cut, peel, blanch, can, freeze, and (in recent years) mostly give away—with neighbors and coworkers cashing in on my penchant for planting. It's hard to believe that seeds barely filling a lunch bag spend a few weeks blending God's creative magic of sun, soil, and water into a winter's worth of food for a family. But that's what seed is all about. Abundant life encased in a tiny, hard shell.

No mere book can deliver full-grown, harvested produce—though some come close. Like seeds, books contain a grain of truth encased in the crusty shell of words. But plant that seed in the right season in a mind ready to learn, tug out the weeds of distraction that disrupt study, water it with a sweated-out attempt to put its truths into practice, invite with prayer the sunshine of God's grace, and expect a crop—enough to nurture personal growth, enough to give away.

What harvest can we expect from TruthSeed?

We can expect to know Scripture. Each book in this series invites us to explore either a topic addressed in several biblical passages or to study an entire book of the Bible. These are inductive studies. Each session leads us to explore a single passage on three levels: details of information presented in the text, accurate interpretation of that information, and personal response.

We can expect to experience God's presence. Scripture points us to God, its author and its object. It is His letter to us about Himself. As we read, study, and meditate on Scripture we will become more and more aware of God. We will see His love and wrath, His mercy and justice, acted out on the pages of these ancient texts. And we will know more and more about God's personal care for us and His desire for us to respond to Him.

We can expect to improve our relationships. Human nature is remarkably resilient; over the millennia we have changed little. Scripture shows us brothers who hate each other enough to kill, and friends who love each other more than their own lives. It shows us the grief of death and the joy of birth. It shows us the celebration of marriage and the pain of marriage ended. It pictures overwhelming generosity and the grudging hunger of greed. It echoes our hopeless moans at life's futility and it shouts our hope for life beyond this life. As Scripture increases our understanding of each other, we can expect to see its fruit wherever we touch other people: at work, in friendships, at churches, in neighborhoods, in casual encounters with waitresses and store clerks, and in the most challenging of all relationships — our families.

We can expect to better understand ourselves. Scripture is an intensely personal book. True, we may read it for historical content, or for its quality literature, or for its insightful teachings. But if Scripture is to accomplish its true purpose, we must read its pages, open ourselves, and allow it to read our souls. Scripture will show us our faults: the jealous brother, the greedy servant, the pompous keeper of laws. But as we let Scripture do its work, we will grow more and more according to God's design: the forgiving parent, the faithful leader, the wise friend, the one who models the love of Jesus Christ. And we will find the empty, God-shaped hole inside being filled by Christ Himself. Even people who don't believe much of what the Bible says, who are turned off by sermons and essays, can appreciate the questions here that allow them to examine the biblical text for themselves, explore its potential meanings, and form personal conclusions about response.

TruthSeed is appropriate for small group discussion or for personal use. Its blend of academic, personal, and relational tasks make it ideal for cell groups, workplace study groups, neighborhood groups, school-based groups, Sunday School classes, retreats, and outreach groups. It is also for personal study, meditation, and growth.

Suggestions for Group Discussion

1. There's no need to be a Bible expert to participate in a TruthSeed discussion. You may find experts in your group, but there is plenty of room for non-experts as well. Since the discussion centers around a single passage, you will all participate on a similar level. And God can grow any of us.

2. Arrive on time—out of consideration for other group members. Bring your TruthSeed guide and a Bible.

3. Commit to regular attendance. Understanding of the Scripture and relationships within the group are cumulative. You and others will benefit most if you can count on each other to be there. If you must be absent, call your host or leader ahead of time.

4. Discussion is a shared responsibility. It blends talking and listening in even balance. If you are a born listener, act on your responsibility to share your insights by making the extra effort necessary. If you are a born talker, sharpen your listening skills by keeping track of the flow of conversation. If you discover that you are "on stage" more than the average person present, shorten your comments and use them to draw other people into the conversation.

5. Treat other group members with respect. You cannot possibly agree with every comment throughout the course of a discussion study. Disagreement is one way to help each other grow toward the truth. But express your disagreement in kind terms that reflect a genuine respect for the person.

6. Guard the privacy of people in your group. Since spiritual growth makes a deep impact on our personal lives, you will likely hear others speak of their private feelings and events. And you may want to speak some of your own private thoughts. Agree together that you will not divulge each other's stories.

7. Don't gossip. Many groups pray together for a variety of needy people. It's tempting to get specific about names and weaknesses in a way that invites more speculation than prayer. Don't do it. It's possible to pray for a person with very little inside information. God knows it anyway.

8. Be willing to discuss the application questions. Some people are content to keep a group study at a purely academic level, so they read the questions that invite personal response, and pass on with the quick instruction to "think about it." But if Scripture is to be more than a textbook of information, we must allow it to penetrate our lives. Members of a group can nurture each other toward spiritual growth as they discuss together its personal impact.

9. Take note of the follow-up assignments. Each TruthSeed study ends with supplementary material that can provide further enrichment. In some cases, this section may prove as valuable as the rest of the study. So take advantage of this added resource.

10. Consider leading a discussion. Many groups rotate leadership so that almost everyone takes a turn asking the questions. This job does not require a lot of special skills, but a few pointers won't hurt. If it's your turn to lead, you will find helps for leaders beginning on page 43.

Suggestions for Personal Study

1. Settle into your favorite "quiet time" spot. Bring your Bible, the TruthSeed guide, writing materials, and (if you like) a commentary or Bible dictionary.

2. Pray. Ask God to reveal Himself to you as you study. Ask that He assist your understanding, that He bare your inner self to His gaze, and that He use your time to bring healing to your relationships.

3. Begin by reading the chapter introduction. Make notes about the first question and allow it to help you approach the topic you are about to study.

4. Read the assigned biblical text. If textual accuracy is one of your priorities, use a contemporary translation (not a paraphrase) that reflects recent scholarship. Mark significant words or phrases in your Bible, draw lines between ideas that seem connected, write questions or comments in the margins. Try reading aloud. It's one of the best ways to keep your mind from wandering.

5. Work through the list of questions. Jot notes in the space provided. Keep a journal of answers that require more space or more lengthy personal reflection.

6. Stop for periods of silence and meditation throughout your quiet time to allow God to work in your inner being.

7. Continue to pray as you study, asking God to reveal what He wants you to know of yourself and of Himself. Read aloud sections of the passage as a prayer inserting "I" and "me" where appropriate—or insert the name of someone you care about.

8. Don't feel that you must do an entire lesson at a single sitting. Feel free to break at natural division points or whenever you have "had enough" for now. Then come back on a different day, reread the text, review your work thus far, and pick up where you left off.

9. When you have completed your personal study of the questions, turn to the appropriate leader's notes in the back of the guide to gain further information you may have missed. If you are the studious type, refer to a commentary or Bible dictionary for more insights. The reading list at the end of the book provides a list of reliable resources.

10. Put the follow-up activities at the end of each study into practice. Read, sing, pray, do, meditate, journal, make the phone call, start the project, repair the relationship. When your study time is finished, God's work in your life has just begun. Allow His work to continue throughout the week.

As you use this TruthSeed guide, I pray that seeds of truth from God's Word will grow a rich harvest in your life.

—Carolyn Nystrom, Editor

Introducing 1 Timothy

Picture yourself in a dimly-lit attic digging through a musty trunk handed down through generations of your family. You find a long letter, open the fragile paper, hold it gently at the edges, and begin to read. Your mind buzzes with questions: Who wrote it? To whom? When? Why? Slowly the letter itself begins to address your questions. Through it you see a past era, peopled by members of your own family, struggling with issues not unlike your own. The Book of 1 Timothy is this kind of letter.

In this letter we see the first-century church (our ancient brothers and sisters) led by Timothy, a young pastor who is counseled by an aging missionary/teacher/theologian: the Apostle Paul. In the Ephesus area where Timothy lived, Christian believers probably met in homes and came together only occasionally as a large congregation. In that era, the church was still trying to get its theology straight (when has it not?) and was therefore easy prey for strange, erroneous teachings. Some of these errors were deliberate—an authoritative person trying to gain a power base. Other errors crept in by mistake—some new believer, uneducated and uninformed, teaching a bit too soon. These first-century Christians came from a variety of other religions or perhaps no religion at all. Understanding the Christian faith came slowly—and sometimes lacked precision.

Yet they were a church. They met together for worship, so they had to decide its form and content. They had to select leaders and define their roles within the congregation, a role quite different than what they occupied in the outside world where some were slaves and others were masters. The people of this church also took care of each other, but they had to decide who should receive the care of the church—and who should give it, and who should simply take care of themselves. Overshadowing all of these decisions about the inner-workings of the church was teaching: What is false teaching? What is true teaching? And how could they maintain what is true?

As with many old family letters, the issues carry through the years.

We too need to find and define our role in the church. We too have to create appropriate worship. We too have to guard the truth. So we ask questions like: How can we create a good worship service when our people have differing tastes in music? How should I function as a worker and an elder—if my boss is in my church? Is it all right for a woman to lead public prayers? To preach? Should we pay the pastor but not the organist? How about the guitar player? How can we find and select capable church leaders? What should the church do if one of its leaders has a moral lapse? If someone begins to teach what is less than Christian? Should we give extra weight to the opinions of people who give a lot of money? Is the church to function as a welfare agency? How can I maintain my own spiritual growth among a group of Christians who are as flawed as I?

The letter of 1 Timothy may not answer all of these questions, but it will help provide principles from which you can create answers. I hope that this guide will help to bring 1 Timothy to life for you in new ways. If you want to read further family letters from the same attic trunk, study the books of 2 Timothy and Titus. You will find similar themes further developed. Together these three books are called the Pastoral Letters. One final note regarding the phrasings of biblical texts in this guide—I have used the NRSV, a fairly new translation. If you are not firmly settled on some other translation, I urge you to try it. If you are studying with a group, others may also enjoy this fresh way of expressing the ancient text. I pray God's best for you as you listen to what God has to say to you through your study of 1 Timothy.

—Scott Hotaling

1
The Heart of the Gospel

1 Timothy 1:1-11

When I was growing up in Kansas, I heard a legend about a church that has always served as sort of a negative model for me. It seems that in this church the piano was situated on the eastern side of the sanctuary. For some forgotten reason, a group of church members were convinced that the piano would be more strategically placed if it were on the western side of the sanctuary. After several months of debate within the church, the western party decided to take matters into its own hands. Late one Saturday night, several of them entered the church and moved the piano. The next morning those who wanted the piano on the eastern side were understandably upset, but could not do anything without making a scene.

The next week several members showed up early Saturday evening to move the piano back to the east. Each week after that the piano was moved several times on Saturday and early Sunday morning. Eventually, the stress of wondering who was going to move it and when became too great. The church split down the middle, with those favoring the west in one group, and those favoring the east in another. According to the story, former members of the church who disagreed still refuse to speak to one another.

While this story is ludicrous, it nevertheless illustrates a number of dangers that we face as Christians, not the least of which is the amount of energy and time that we spend on things that have little or nothing to do with the central aspects of the Gospel.

1. What problems can happen when we get distracted from the core of the Gospel?

2. What are some safeguards that God has given to keep us focused on what is important about our faith?

Read aloud 1 Timothy 1:1-11

3. What do the first two verses tell you about the writer and recipient of this letter?

4. Survey the rest of the passage. Which words here have strong positive content?

Now list all the words in the passage that carry strong negative content.

5. Paul usually opened his letters with a prayer of thanks and praise to God, but in this letter he jumps right into his message. What might have motivated him to do this?

6. Look more carefully at verses 3-7. What descriptions does Paul give of false doctrine and those who teach it?

7. In verse 3, Paul told Timothy to instruct these people not to teach. Why? (Take a careful look at verse 5.)

8. In verse 6, Paul speaks of "meaningless talk." Why is it that the sort of love Paul refers to in verse 5 cannot exist where there is meaningless talk?

9. What kinds of "meaningless talk" can keep *you* from loving others?

10. Focus on verses 8-11. In verse 7, Paul complains that these problem people want to be "teachers of the law"—but that they don't understand it themselves. In verse 8, he says that the law is good if it is used "legitimately." How have you seen God's law used in a wrong way?

11. How does the list in verses 9-10 compare to the Ten Commandments?

12. In verses 9-11, Paul lists a variety of types of sinners; in fact, few people are able to completely escape the list. What do you think is the function of the law for those who find themselves on the list?

13. Judging from the first eleven verses of this book, what would you say are the reason or reasons Paul had for writing this letter to Timothy?

14. You began this study by thinking about ways that we get distracted from the real core of the Gospel. Paul expresses part of that core in verse 5. What kinds of help do you personally need to have a "love that comes from a pure heart, a good conscience, and sincere faith"?

Now or Later

✦ Try to be extra-sensitive to the temptations you face to participate in activities that distract you from how God would have you spend your time and energy. If you find journaling helpful, make a note of the more obvious examples.

✦ Whether or not you journal, share with another Christian your observations about where you are facing temptation. Then help each other keep the core of your faith consistent with your actions by agreeing to check with each other on a regular basis.

2
The Worst Sinner

1 Timothy 1:12-20

He was a hardened gang member, tattooed, and tough-talking. He had seen "action" that most of us witness only on TV crime shows. Yet he had turned from his past and given his life to Christ. His leather jacket, motorcycle, and serpent tattoo were only surface reminders of the radical inner change. He was a seminary student just like me—hungry to reach others with the good news he had heard.

Perhaps you know someone who has experienced a radical turnaround through meeting Christ. We often tend to notice the conversions of these—the worst of sinners. In truth, however, any one of us who comes to Christ can count ourselves as needing radical transformation—whether it is from gossiping, lying, shady business deals, or materialism.

The Apostle Paul, who counts himself as "the worst of sinners," has had just such a life-changing meeting with Christ. He encourages us that we can experience Christ's mercy—just as he did.

1. How do you react when you hear about someone notorious, like Manuel Noriega (who had a prison conversion), becoming a Christian?

Read aloud 1 Timothy 1:12-20

2. Describe the picture that Paul paints of Jesus in this passage.

What words are keys to seeing this picture?

3. What positive and negative words does Paul use to describe himself in verses 12-16?

4. It would be an understatement to say that Paul had a life-changing experience of conversion. Briefly describe the turn-around in Paul's life as seen in these verses.

5. In verse 13 Paul states, "I received mercy because I had acted ignorantly in unbelief." What difference did it make that he acted in ignorance and unbelief?

6. How is your experience of Jesus similar to Paul's conversion?

How is it different?

7. Meditate for a moment on the doxology of verse 17. What do you find here that would aid your worship of God?

8. Paul says in verse 12 that Christ has strengthened him, so he can reasonably tell Timothy in verse 18 to "fight the good fight." When have you felt that the Christian life was a battle?

9. Verse 19 says that Hymenaeus and Alexander rejected their consciences. What dangers would you worry about if you thought someone in your own church had rejected his or her conscience?

10. What is the purpose of Hymenaeus and Alexander being "turned over to Satan"?

11. What sorts of actions or beliefs do you think are offenses serious enough to deserve some sort of exclusion from today's church?

12. Accountability means allowing each other to help us keep our commitments to follow Christ. How can members of your own church (or group) better hold each other accountable to reflect the attributes of Jesus outlined in verses 12-16? (Try to think of two or three specific ways.)

Now or Later

✦ Meditate on God as He is described in the doxology of verse 17. (Look also at Psalm 18:1-3.) Then select one aspect of God from this doxology and pray your own prayer of praise for that quality. You may want to first write out your prayer and then read it to God. Sample prayer: "Lord, I praise you for _____ because . . ."

✦ Working in pairs or all together, suggest ways that you might like to be held accountable by others in the group. Pray for one another. Follow up in future studies by asking each other how you are doing.

3
Politically Correct?

1 Timothy 2:1-15

A friend of mine tells of arriving at a Bible study meeting in which this passage — especially verses 11-15 — was to be discussed. She was one of the last to arrive, and when she walked into the room she noticed that the women in the study were all sitting on one side of the room, and the men were all sitting on the other side. She knew then that the ensuing discussion was not likely to be boring.

In today's passage, the Apostle Paul speaks his mind about some pressing issues in the church of his day. Of course, Paul was neither a Rush Limbaugh nor a Phil Donahue. Issues of political correctness were not part of his experience. He probably never imagined the kinds of debates that rage on our college campuses, in political arenas, on television, and even in our churches.

Sometimes we who are in the church feel that we should not voice our opinions because they might be divisive. As Christians, however, it's important that we learn to communicate and work through our differences. You may or may not always like what Paul has to say, but read and consider carefully how you need to interpret and apply it to your context. You may be surprised.

1. Have you ever had a friend that you disagreed with in some significant area? How did you work through the differences?

19

2. What experiences have you had with women being in leadership positions — in church, community, work, or family settings?

How did you feel about the situation?

Read aloud 1 Timothy 2:1-15

3. Imagine that the Apostle Paul has just been among you, and spoken the words you have just heard. Which of his comments got your attention the most?

4. What was your reaction to what he had to say?

5. What are the purposes of prayer for everyone in verses 1-4?

6. What do we learn about God the Father and Christ the Son from verses 3-7?

7. What implications for your life can you draw from what we know about God in this passage?

8. This chapter seems to be primarily concerned with what happened in worship or prayer meetings in the church at Ephesus. In view of his instructions, what were the practices and attitudes that Paul found troubling? (verses 8-12)

   How do you think the instructions here might relate to the teaching problem that Paul began to address in the first chapter? (See especially verses 3-7.)

9. What would concern Paul about prayer or worship in your own church?

10. In verses 11-14, Paul states in strong terms his position and reasoning on the place of a woman in a church's worship, teaching, and leadership. What impact do you think these verses should have on the role of a woman in today's church?

11. How does your church handle the role of women in leadership?

Do you agree or disagree with its approach? Explain.

Now or Later

You may want to explore this topic further. If you are meeting with a group, one way of further exploration would be to schedule a future study in which members of the group research and present several different perspectives on the issue for discussion. *Women in Ministry: Four Views*, edited by Robert and Bonnidell Clouse (InterVarsity Press), outlines four common views. You may want to assign individuals or partners to each of these perspectives.

✦ *Traditional:* Women are not to be involved in ministry.

✦ *Male leadership:* Women can have limited involvement as long as they are under the direction of a male pastor.

✦ *Plural ministry:* All believers are ministers — overemphasizing ordination creates arguments over women's roles.

✦ *Egalitarian:* Woman should engage in any kind of service for which they are gifted and to which they feel called.

4
Beyond Reproach

1 Timothy 3:1-13

One of the running jokes of my college and seminary years — when I was still single — was that anyone going into the ministry should avoid dating someone who wanted to be a pastor's spouse. The assumption was that a person who had that wish was either masochistic or extremely naive.

This attitude became prevalent because, in the past at least, there has been a multitude of expectations concerning pastors, their wives, and their children. While people would rarely say something as explicit as, "Our pastor should be a better Christian than the rest of us," many Christians have long felt that pastors — and other church leaders — should be different in meaningful ways.

Often this has meant unbearable expectations for pastors and their families. But at the heart of those sometimes unreasonable assumptions is a biblical concern: there are (or should be) requirements for church leaders.

1. In your experience, what are some of the things that are expected (spoken or unspoken) of church leaders and their families?

2. What might be the source of some of these expectations?

Read aloud 1 Timothy 3:1-13

3. Paul describes more than thirty requirements for bishops, deacons, and women. (The "women" were either deacons or the wives of deacons.) What are these church leaders to be — and not be? (Find all that you can.)

4. Select one spiritual leader that you know. Describe how this person lives out one of the positive qualities in this passage.

5. In verse 1, Paul says that the office of bishop is a noble task. How does this fit with your experience of the assumptions made about church leaders?

   How does "noble task" compare with the expectations and assumptions of the secular world about Christian leaders?

6. The word "bishop" in verse 2 is translated "leader" in *Good News Bible* and *New English Bible;* and "overseer" in *New International Version.* Paul says that a bishop must be above reproach. Do you think this means that a bishop is someone who is chosen because that person is above reproach, or that a

person who is chosen to be a bishop should behave so as to be above reproach? Explain.

7. Paul lists ten other characteristics of bishops in verses 2-3. How do these qualities help a church leader to be effective?

8. In verse 5, Paul compares the management of a household to the care of God's church. What parallels have you seen between relationships in a family and relationships in a church?

9. In verses 6-7, Paul gives two examples of how those in positions of power fall into temptation. What effects are likely when a church leader is overcome by evil forces?

What are some other examples of how leaders experience spiritual battles?

10. In verse 8, Paul says that deacons are not to be double-tongued. What does he mean?

11. Deacons are also to "hold fast to the mystery of the faith" (verse 9). When is it hard for you to hold fast to faith?

12. Verse 10 outlines an intensive selection process for deacons. What are some ways that we can implement this kind of process in our churches today?

13. How does taking on Christian responsibility help us grow in faith?

14. Whether or not you are in a position of leadership, what do you need to do to ensure that you are above reproach?

Now or Later

✦ With your group, make a list of church leaders that various members work with. If the group is part of a larger church body, include also denominational or regional leaders. Take a few minutes to pray for these leaders.

✦ Brainstorm ways that members of the group can encourage and help your church leaders in the coming weeks.

✦ Choose a particular church leader to pray for in the future. Try to find at least one tangible way to show your support for that person during the next week.

5
True Religion

1 Timothy 3:14–4:5

I n the last section of the Disney classic, *Fantasia*, the storytellers take two very different pieces of music, "Night on Bald Mountain," by Mussorgsky and Schubert's "Ave Maria," and set them against each other. In the first movement, the animated mountain comes to life as either a hideous demon, or perhaps the devil himself, and wreaks havoc on the town below. The animators draw wraiths, fiery pits, demons riding the skeletons of horses, and various other visual horrors to communicate an intense sense of the power and presence of evil.

As the heavy, dark music of "Night on Bald Mountain" gives way to the light strains of the "Ave Maria," the animation changes to pilgrims making their way through the night on a difficult journey. With the eventual triumph of the music, the pilgrims enter a valley just at the moment of the rising of the sun, and the beginning of a new day. The second half of the story only works because the audience has first seen the horror and reality of evil.

In this passage, we will see the Apostle Paul do just the opposite— but with the same effect. He first shows the beauty of true religion, and only then does he expose the ugliness of the false religion of his opponents.

1. Have you ever known someone who was drawn into a cult or a Christian group with cultic elements? Describe the situation or group.

27

2. What do you think draws people into cultic groups?

Read aloud 1 Timothy 3:14–4:5

3. According to 1 Timothy 3:14-16, what is true religion?

4. In chapter 4, verses 1-3, Paul comments on the false religion of the false teachers. What differences do you notice between this and the true religion he describes in 3:14-16?

5. According to verses 14-15, what is the purpose of the letter?

   How does this connect with the purpose put forth in 1 Timothy 1:3-7?

6. Verse 16 is a glorious proclamation of Christ. Take a few minutes and, line by line, comment on what each of the six lines of this Christ-hymn means to you.

7. What can we know about the work of the false teachers from 1 Timothy 4:1-3?

8. What is Paul's response to the specific false teachings named in verse 3? (Study verses 4-5.)

9. How can an overly strict view of what is and is not permitted by God be dangerous to our faith?

How would you compare this danger to the danger of being too permissive with God's law? (Do you think one danger is greater than the other?)

10. What guidelines do we have to determine whether or not something that is not specifically evil is worth doing?

11. What practices and possessions do you think you feel false guilt about?

12. How would you like to enjoy the good things God has created this week?

Now or Later

Fantasia is not a Christian movie, yet it offers a creative depiction of true versus false religion. What medium could you use to celebrate true religion—and perhaps show how it contrasts with false religion? Consider drawing or painting, putting together pieces of music you find meaningful (not necessarily your own composition; it could even be prerecorded), making a chart or graph, clay modeling, and so on. You might want to do one of these as a group or bring individual projects back next week.

6
Godly
Training

1 Timothy 4:6-16

My senior year in college I gave a formal recital with a friend. Although I had often performed piano solos publicly, I had never sung a formal solo. But I had been taking voice lessons for a year and a half, so I decided to both play and sing. I remember preparing for the recital. I practiced and I worried; I practiced and I got scared; I practiced and I practiced. But most of all, I remember my friends who kept encouraging me to go through with it. They knew as well as I did that no one would get goosebumps listening to me sing. But they also knew that I wanted to do it, and no one would think less of me for doing my best.

When the night of the performance finally came, I did okay. No one offered me a singing contract, but I knew that I had done my best. And the friends who had encouraged me before the recital, pointed out all the things I had done well.

In this passage, Paul encourages Timothy to work and train himself—in order to fulfill his calling as a minister of Christ. Timothy no doubt needed encouragement and prodding just as much as I did.

1. Describe ways that have you "trained" for something—like a test, a new job, or a race?

What have you found rewarding, and what have you found frustrating about this kind of training?

Read aloud 1 Timothy 4:6-16

2. In this passage Paul turns his attention to Timothy personally. List all of the friendly commands Paul has for Timothy in these verses.

3. Imagine that you are Timothy, and have just read these verses, written by your friend and mentor, Paul the apostle. What is your reaction to his commands and encouragements?

4. Who are your spiritual mentors? That is, who has encouraged you in your Christian training? How?

5. In verse 7, Paul tells Timothy to have nothing to do with "profane myths and old wives' tales." In view of your study in this letter so far, what myths and tales might Paul be talking about?

What are some "profane myths and old wives' tales" that circulate in today's church and society?

6. In verses 7 and 8, Paul says that godliness is valuable because it holds "promise for both the present life and the life to come." In what ways have you seen godliness to be valuable in the present life?

7. Paul tells Timothy to "train yourself in godliness." Why? (Study verses 7-11.)

What are some ways that you could (or do) train yourself in godliness?

8. Verse 12 says that Timothy is to be an example. What ways of leading by example do you spot in verses 12-16? (Find all that you can.)

9. Several times throughout this letter, Paul has expressed his concern for godly teaching. What relationships do you see here between leading by teaching and leading by example?

10. All believers are spiritual leaders to someone — perhaps even to children. What instructions here are important for you to incorporate into your own leadership? How and why?

11. Throughout this passage Paul has encouraged Timothy—even referred once again (in verse 14) to "the gift that is in you." How have other Christians affirmed your gifts and encouraged you to use them?

When are you tempted to neglect your gifts?

12. Take a moment to name the gifts and talents that you see in several friends or family members. Create an opportunity to express appreciation of those skills in the coming week. If you are meeting in a group, mention a skill or talent that you appreciate in the person on your right. Then suggest ways that this person can or does use that ability for God.

Now or Later

Do you know what your spiritual gifts are? All of our skills and abilities come from God, but the Bible lists several specific gifts that we can use as we serve God. These lists appear in Romans 12:3-8, 1 Corinthians 12:4-11 and Ephesians 4:8-12. The list in Romans is a good, concise summary. Here they are with brief definitions:

+ *Prophecy:* Confronting sin and calling people to repent. Billy Graham may be an example of one who exercises this gift.
+ *Serving:* Who in your church is always the first one there setting up chairs or the last one to leave because there are dishes to be washed? These humble people probably have the gift of service.
+ *Teaching:* The ability to interpret and communicate God's word to others. John Stott comes to mind here.

+ *Encouraging:* This person is able to come alongside others and help them along. The encourager can see the gifts and abilities in others and show them how to use them.
+ *Giving:* We are all called to give of our time and resources, but there are some who lead the way for us. Who in your church has a vision for giving?
+ *Mercy:* I think of a woman at church who often tears up when she hears of people in pain. Those who show mercy are able to deeply identify with the pain of others.
+ *Leading:* Those who guide and direct a church or organization so that the ministry is growing and effective have the gift of leadership. Jimmy Carter may be an example of this as he teaches his Sunday School class and leads his *Habitat for Humanity* program.

Study and pray over the lists of God's gifts mentioned in the texts above. Then evaluate your specific interests and skills—even though they may not appear in one of these lists. Many skills are closely related to the general categories. For example, a person skilled in auto mechanics or plumbing may use those skills as the gift of "helps." Ask God to reveal your spiritual gifts to you. Ask others what they see as your gifts so that they can confirm (or question) your understanding of God's leading

7
Honoring the Needy

1 Timothy 5:1-16

A church was having its annual meeting. They enjoyed a meal together. They recognized church staff and Sunday School teachers. Then they celebrated the commitment of the church community by reading the church's covenant. One part of that covenant was a pledge to help those who are in physical or emotional need — both within the church and the surrounding community.

Present at that meeting was a woman with some significant needs. She was physically disabled. She came from an abusive home and had lost contact with all of her family members. She had recently moved into a new place, but hadn't been able to get all of her belongings moved. She was living in an apartment with a mattress and a few boxes. Was anyone available to help her? No. It was a busy time in the life of the church.

Does this sound familiar? All too often people in churches try to change the world around them, without taking care of those already in the body of Christ. Paul found it necessary to address some of the same problems in the church in Ephesus.

1. Have you ever been in a situation in which you felt separated from family and friends — for example, moving to a new place, attending a conference, or being overseas? What was that experience like for you?

Read aloud 1 Timothy 5:1-16

2. What relationships does Paul write about in these verses?

3. What responsibilities go with each of the relationships?

4. How does the way in which we speak to someone reflect how we regard them? (See verses 1 and 2.)

5. Who are the "real widows" according to verses 3-8?

How might the instructions here affect your own sense of family responsibility?

6. According to verses 9 and 10, what requirements must be met before a widow is "put on the list"?

7. Focus on verses 11-15. What special concerns does Paul have about young widows? Why?

8. Why do you think Paul specifies the type of widow who should be helped?

9. What principles does this suggest about who your church should offer to help?

10. Who are the people in our society that are helpless like the "real widows" of Ephesus?

What examples of this kind of need do you see in your neighborhood, town, or church?

11. What can the church do to provide support and help for those in need?

What can *you* do?

Now or Later

Paul begins verse 3 by saying that we are to "honor" widows. Do you *honor* the needy people you know? Consider your attitude toward them and how you regard their needs. Reflect on the situation you recalled in the opening question. Make your attitude (and then your actions) a matter of prayer.

8
A Double Honor

1 Timothy 5:17–6:2a

Frank was the pastor of a small, rural church. After several years of trying (with mixed results) to build relationships in the church, he was burned out. In his depression he had an affair with a woman in the church. When members of the church found out about the affair, there was no accountability and reconciliation structure in place. So both families involved, along with several other significant members, felt they had no choice but to leave the church.

Frank left that church and got help. He was in counseling for a couple of years. He became accountable to a group of Christian men and met with them regularly. He and his wife were able to put the pain of the affair behind them and re-create their marriage. Eventually a new church, knowing of the affair at the previous church, called him to ministry. For a time, things went well. Then, rumors from the old church started spreading to members of the new church. Some people, not directly involved, said that there had been other immoralities throughout Frank's years of ministry. These accusation were unfair—and untrue. But they caused Frank and his family to relive all the pain of the past. And they sowed doubts among the new congregation.

1. How have you been hurt by Christian leaders who have betrayed your trust, or by Christian groups who have "devoured" their leaders?

2. What results, both immediately and in the long run, came from these incidents?

Read 1 Timothy 5:17–6:2a

3. As a group, or individually, create a visual representation of Paul's line of thinking in this passage. You can make a map, graph, or whatever captures the flow of the passage.

4. According to verses 17-18, what all is included in the double honor to be given to elders who rule well?

5. What is the basis for financial support of church leaders?

6. In verses 19-20, Paul addresses the problem of elders who sin or seem to sin. What types of danger is Paul trying to avoid with his instructions in these verses?

7. Why do you think Paul gives these special instructions for the sins of the elders?

8. At times well-known Christian leaders have been accused (sometimes unjustly) of teaching heresy. In view of Paul's instructions here, what responsibilities do you think we have to examine the teachings of Christian leaders?

9. In verse 21, Paul warns Timothy to carry out these instructions without prejudice and not on the basis of partiality. What people do you find it difficult to deal fairly with, especially when you suspect they may have done something wrong?

10. In verse 22, what does Paul mean when he warns Timothy to "not participate in the sins of others?"

11. Timothy is apparently suffering from stomach disorders, perhaps because of poor water, so Paul suggests drinking wine. What does this tell you about the importance of physical health in relationship to morals?

12. In verses 24-25, Paul speaks of sin and of good works. In what ways are they similar? Why?

13. What principles for honoring those who are in authority over you can you draw from 6:1-2a?

Suppose that slave was an elder in his master's church. In that situation, why might the teachings here be especially difficult — and important?

14. How has seeing someone's good work, as mentioned in verse 25, encouraged you recently?

How can you express appreciation for that good work?

Now or Later

In 1 Timothy 5:19-20, Paul gives some instructions for accountability. How are you doing with accountability within your group? If you have not felt ready to do this, consider it again. (You may want to review some of the work in Study 2.) Pray for one another, and be sure to follow up in future weeks.

9
The Good Fight

1 Timothy 6:2b-16

Paul and Timothy lived in a time when the good fight for faith was clearly defined. There was often a price to pay for following Jesus. Much was at stake. Yet, Paul chooses in this letter not to warn Timothy about the dangers of being thrown to the lions, or of Roman soldiers throwing him into jail, or even of being ridiculed in the streets of Ephesus. Instead, Paul warns Timothy of those who would pervert the Gospel from within, of those who would use the Gospel for their own gain, of those who would cause trouble and dissension.

We also live in a culture which is increasingly hostile to the Christian claim that Jesus is the only way to God. Government agencies allow churches less and less room to function. One church in Washington, D.C. was told that its ministry to the homeless was not tax exempt because feeding the hungry "is not part of the church's mission." I know of another instance in which a government agency tried to force a charitable Christian organization to hire non-Christians. And I certainly remember being laughed at in school for being "good." Yet in the midst of this is the ever-present danger that those within the church will do more damage to the Gospel than those on the outside.

1. When have you seen the Gospel perverted or made into a tool for the gain of individuals?

Read aloud 1 Timothy 6:2b-16

2. According to this passage, what does Paul think is important in life?

   What are the things that are unimportant?

3. What tests does Paul give in verse 3 to identify the false teachers?

4. This seems to be Paul's final big attack on the false teachers. What new information do we learn about them in verses 3-5?

5. According to verses 6-8, how can we find contentment in life?

6. When (and why) are you likely to be discontented?

7. In verses 9-10, Paul speaks of the special temptations of wealth. When have you seen people destroyed by the love of money?

   In view of the warnings in verses 9-10, what counsel would you offer to a wealthy Christian who does not want his or her money to cause spiritual downfall?

8. The command in verse 12 to "fight the good fight" also appears in 1:18. Why do you think Paul emphasizes this with Timothy?

9. According to verses 11-14, what is required to "fight the good fight"?

   What aspect of the good fight do you most need to focus on?

10. In much of the letter Paul focuses on Christ's humanity. How does this contrast with the picture of God in verses 13-16?

11. How would this description of the holiness and power of God have been an encouragement to Timothy?

   How do these same words encourage you?

12. How have you had to fight to maintain your faith?

   What helped you in the fight?

Now or Later

As a group or individually, think of songs that help you to focus on what is important in life, that help you to keep striving to do God's will. In the coming week, each person should try to focus on one song that someone else suggested, and pray for that person each time the song comes to mind.

10
Using Our Riches

1 Timothy 6:17-21

I had never been in a house like this. Spiral staircase, oak trim, spacious rooms, state-of-the-art kitchen — even a heated floor. Situated in a secluded area, this house was what I thought of as a mansion. And the owners were Christians.

I also knew that the owners were major donors to a Christian organization with a ministry to the poor. They were generous in sharing their home with the ministry. They truly desired to help further the work through their gifts of both time and money.

Yet as I walked through the perfectly decorated house, I thought of the question that Tony Campolo has often asked: "Would Jesus drive a BMW?" In the same way, I wondered whether a Christian should be this rich.

1. What are some of the questions and feelings that you have had about the relationship between wealth and Christianity?

Read aloud 1 Timothy 6:17-21

2. What cautions do you find here about wealth?

What responsibilities?

3. How does "the uncertainty of riches" contrast with God's provisions described in verses 17 and 19?

4. In verse 17, Paul cautions the wealthy not to be haughty. In what situations do you have to battle being "haughty" about what you have been given?

5. According to verse 18, the rich are to do four things. Why are they given these specific commands?

6. Try for a moment to see your own possessions through the eyes of a Christian from an impoverished country. (Consider the place where you live, your closet, your refrigerator or pantry, your transportation.) What would this person find surprising?

What questions do you think this person would ask about the relationship between your possessions and your faith?

7. Tony Campolo has said that if all Christians tithed (gave away ten percent of their income) world hunger could be eliminated. How can our riches help us to live out the commands Paul gives to the rich in verse 18?

8. Verse 17 says that God "richly provides us with everything for our enjoyment." As quickly as possible, name five gifts from God that you enjoy. (They need not cost much money. *Enjoyment*, not value, is the issue.)

9. In verse 20 Paul tells Timothy to guard what has been entrusted to him. What have you been entrusted with? (Draw from all of 1 Timothy.)

   How could you make better use of what you have been entrusted with?

10. Focus on verses 20-21. Describe the kinds of people Paul is warning Timothy against.

    How have you seen Christians led astray by people like this?

11. What have you learned from 1 Timothy about who God wants you to be?

What steps of progress are you making (or can you make) in that direction?

12. Close by thanking God for the gifts He has given you—and for the capacity to enjoy them.

Now or Later

Where do you as a group want to go from here? 1 Timothy may have opened a number of areas of interest you could pursue. Possible follow-up topics include: how we are to love one another in the church, developing Christian character, who Christ is, spiritual gifts, Christian leadership, roles in the church, Christian doctrine. Plan to spend your next session examining various study guides together to decide what would be best for your group to use next.

Notes for Leaders

Preparation

Begin your preparation with prayer and personal study. Prepare to lead your particular lesson by following the ten steps under *Suggestions for Personal Study* beginning on page 7.

Study the biblical context of the passage under consideration. Research any questions likely to sidetrack your group.

Study the flow of questions. TruthSeed questions are designed to create a flow of discussion from beginning to end. Get comfortable with the potential directions of the study. Mark pacing notes so that the discussion will spread evenly over your allotted time. Most TruthSeed studies should last about an hour.

Read the leader's notes for your particular study beginning on page 52. Mark information that you may need during the course of the study in the blank spaces of your question list.

If your group time includes other ingredients such as refreshments, music, worship, sharing, and prayer, plan time divisions so that your group is able to accomplish all that is scheduled. Many TruthSeed lessons make suggestions for these additional ingredients at the close of the Bible study section.

Acknowledge to yourself and to God that the group belongs to the people in it, not to you as a leader. TruthSeed is designed to facilitate a group discovery form of learning moderated by a discussion leader. Plan to lead with the group's welfare and interests in mind.

Pray for each group member by name.

Group Time

Begin on time. No apology necessary. The group has come together for a particular purpose and has assigned you the job of leading it in the study.

If your group is meeting for the first time, survey together the suggestions for group discussion on page 6. This will help each person to know what is expected and will get you off on a common footing.

Take appropriate note of the narrative introduction at the beginning of the study, then ask the opening question. Encourage responses from each person. When everyone seems involved in the subject at hand, the group will be ready to enter the biblical text. Since the opening questions point toward the text but do not interact with it, always ask the opening question BEFORE reading the Scripture.

Read the assigned Scripture passage aloud. Or ask several group members to read. Some people feel embarrassed about their reading skills, so don't make surprise assignments unless you are certain that they will be well accepted. Paragraph breaks in the text mark natural thought divisions, so always read by paragraphs, not by verses.

Conduct a discussion of the biblical text using the questions supplied. TruthSeed questions should promote multiple answers and group interaction. Allow time for several people to respond to each question and to each other. If the group does not seem to understand a particular question, rephrase it until it becomes clear, break it into smaller units, or give a brief summary and move on.

Give encouraging comments. If an answer is partially right, acknowledge that part. If an answer seems inappropriate, say something like, "What verse led you to that conclusion?" or "What do some of the rest of you think?"

Don't be afraid of silence. Help group members to become comfortable with the quiet by announcing a "thinking time." Then invite them to share their thoughtful responses to the questions at hand. Learn a sensitivity to God that can come from occasional silence.

Pace the study. It is the leader's responsibility to be sure that you finish on time and that the group has adequate time to discuss later questions. Some questions will take longer than others, so create a flexible pace with one eye on the clock and the other on interests of your group. Don't be afraid to redirect attention to the question list or the biblical text. Suggest that you may come back to some interesting topic after you have finished the study.

Involve everyone—more or less equally. Draw in quiet people by asking for nonthreatening opinion responses. Avoid direct eye contact with someone who talks a bit too much. If necessary, point out the shared responsibility for a successful discussion by reading item four on page 6.

Avoid over-talking yourself. Groups with an overactive leader get tempted to sit back and let the leader do *all* the work. Eventually, this causes people to lose the benefit of a personal encounter with the Scripture as it impacts their own lives.

Keep the discussion on track. Consider writing the purpose statement from the leader's section at the top of your question page so that you can keep the discussion objective in mind. You can head off a tangent by gently directing attention back to the biblical text. But do consider the relative merit of any potential tangent. Sometimes apparent tangents represent real needs that the group ought to address. In that case, adjust your plan (for the moment) and follow the needs of the group. If the tangent seems of limited interest or importance, offer to talk about it in more detail at a later time. Or if the tangent is of great importance, but requires further preparation, ask the group to table it for this session, but come back to it at a later meeting.

Don't skip questions of personal application. Here is where Scripture does its most important work. As other group members respond, be ready to add your own experiences of God's work in your life.

Open and close your study with prayer. Or ask someone in your group to do so.

Study One
The Heart of the Gospel
1 Timothy 1:1-11

Purpose: To explore ways that we are distracted from the core of the Gospel.

Question 1. Help your group to consider how we may neglect others or fail to express love and concern for them even while trying to "live a Christian life." The core of our faith is following Jesus Christ and loving our neighbors. Be ready to respond to this question with an idea or two of your own in case the group needs help to get going. Then encourage others to add insight.

Question 2. Possible responses include Scripture, the church, Christian friends, the Holy Spirit, prayer, and Christian books.

Question 3. Use this question to help your group note and discuss virtually each word of the first two verses. They are the major clues to authorship, readers, and the relationship between them. If your group wants background information at this point, you can draw from material supplied below.

The group may raise the question of the authorship of the Pastorals. (*The Pastorals* is a group name for 1 and 2 Timothy and Titus.) While these letters claim to be from Paul, many scholars have concluded that all three of the letters were written by someone else—in Paul's name. Such a practice in our situation would be considered fraud, but in the ancient world this would have been acceptable. There are several reasons that some say Paul did not write the Pastoral Letters. Much of the language is different than the rest of Paul's letters. There are several new ideas in the Pastorals not found in Paul's other letters. For example, in the Pastorals faith has become an object to be guarded. In Paul's other writings, faith is something that is always directed toward God in Jesus Christ.

Some scholars (Hanson, for example) believe that the Pastorals were written by someone in the 2nd century and are meant to attack Gnosticism—a heresy which emphasized that special knowledge brought about salvation and that Jesus was not really God. Others such as Barclay have argued that much of the material was written or spoken by Paul, but that this material was collected, edited, and added to by a follower of Paul after his death—to combat people who were perverting Paul's gospel.

I believe, however, that Paul did in fact write the letters (although he likely had a secretary who made editorial changes) to Timothy to combat "false teachers" who had begun to emphasize heretical practices and beliefs. In coming to this position, I am indebted to Gordon Fee and his commentary *1 and 2 Timothy, Titus.* Those who wish to read more on the background of 1 Timothy are encouraged to start with Fee. For those who want a more exhaustive study of the discussion, see Donald Guthrie's *New Testament Introduction.*

Question 4. Quite a few "qualitative" words appear in this passage, so this question may take some time. If possible, help your group to briefly note who or what each item refers to.

Question 5. A quick survey of Paul's various New Testament letters (for example, Romans 1:8, Philippians 1:3-6, and even 2 Timothy 1:3) will show that Paul usually takes a moment to thank or praise God after the greeting. This thanksgiving is often directed at the recipients of the letter in question.

The other glaring exception to this rule is his letter to the Galatians, in which Paul is evidently so distressed about their situation that he is distracted, or perhaps isn't even thankful for them at that point. A parallel situation may have been true for 1 Timothy.

According to Gordon Fee, in the *New International Biblical Commentary* "The absence of [a thanksgiving] here supports the observation . . . that 1 Timothy is really for the sake of the church as much as, or more than, for Timothy himself; what is taking place in the church gives no cause for thanksgiving" (p. 39).

Question 6. Help your group to spot descriptive words throughout verses 3-7. They should spot about ten of these. The "false teachers" were evidently spending a great deal of time in speculation. Scholars are not really sure what these teachers were speculating about. They may have been involved in some sort of Gnostic heresy; that is, attempting, through increased "knowledge," to find new ways to God. Later, full-blown Gnosticism created a hierarchy of spiritual beings who served as a pathway to God through knowledge.

A more likely theory is that the false teachers were caught up in speculations about Jewish concerns, probably about the Law, (see 1 Timothy 1:8-11), which seems to be a response to the speculations of the false teachers. Paul, however, does not really give enough clues here to help us draw definite conclusions. It is also interesting that Paul saves his harshest language for the false teachers until chapter four of the letter.

Question 7. Help your group spend adequate time understanding verse 5. Since much of the rest of this book builds on the problems created by these teachers of false doctrine, it is important to understand Paul's motives for his remaining teachings in the letter. J.B. Phillips has a nicely worded paraphrase of verse 5: "The ultimate aim of the Christian ministry, after all, is to produce the love which springs from a pure heart, a good conscience, and a genuine faith."

Question 8. According to Fee, "The purpose of ordering [the false teachers] to stop is to bring the church back to the proper result of 'God's work, based on faith,' namely, their loving one another" (p. 42). The danger of "meaning-less" talk is not just that it does not accomplish anything, but that it distracts us from doing something positive and "meaning-ful."

Question 9. This question should elicit a response from just about everyone in the group. Stress that there are a variety of appropriate answers. Also, it is possible that one person's "meaningless talk" will be something that is helpful to someone else, so try to avoid sweeping statements.

Although the "meaningless talk" that Paul was referring to was evidently quite "religious," a variety of kinds of talk can be meaningless and distracting from true Christian pursuits. Talk shows about visitors from Venus, conversations with nothing but negative content, church fights over minor points of theology, gossip, even being a couch potato can all be things that distract us from loving each other—we don't necessarily have to talk to participate in "meaningless talk."

Question 11. The list, starting with "for those who kill their father or mother" is a fairly explicit echo of Commandments 5–9, (Exodus 20:12-16).

Question 12. The role of the Law in Paul's thought is not easily understood. At points he clearly sees that no one is able to keep all aspects of the Law—hence lists like we find here that include most people in one way or another—and Paul speaks of it in negative terms. At other times he sees it as a gift from God.

The point here is probably that it is through the Law that we realize our sin and imperfections, and therefore realize our need for grace. The Law also works as an equalizer, in the sense that it shows us that we are all in some sense equal in our inability to keep the Law completely.

It is possible that the false teachers that Paul opposes in the letter were advocating some view of the Law that assumed that keeping the Law could be a way of salvation—apart from the work of Christ.

Question 13. There may be several ideas put forth to answer this question. First Timothy, along with 2 Timothy and Titus, have long been considered to be manuals for church organization or administration. This often leads readers to try to extract sections from the letters and paste them onto the life of a local church. When looking at the study for this passage, however, it seems that Paul wrote the letter to Timothy to encourage and empower him to combat the false teachers. Gordon Fee states, "All the crucial matters that make up the framework and content of 1 Timothy are set out in the opening paragraph (vv. 3-7)" (p. 39). This is not to deny that the letter contains significant sections on church administration, but rather to recognize that those sections are necessary because of the reality of the conflict with the false teachers, who were most likely operating from within the church.

Question 14. This is a good opportunity for significant personal interaction within the group. If members already trust each other, it may be helpful to explore ways that group members can help each other develop these attributes—through prayer, building relationships, and accountability.

Study Two
The Worst Sinner
1 Timothy 1:12-20

Purpose: To understand that Christ offers mercy to us no matter how great or small our sins.

Question 1. Group members may react in several different ways to this question. Some may say that it is not our place to judge what happens between God and another person. Others may show skepticism at such "timely" conversions. I myself remember as a teenager hearing a speaker who was converted out of the '70s drug culture. His description of his life before meeting Jesus was so detailed and interesting that it made that way of living seem preferable to my own stable upbringing. Such "testimonies" can be very dangerous.

Question 2. In this passage Paul gushes about the grace and mercy he received from Jesus. Even though Paul writes this letter years, perhaps even decades, after his conversion, he " . . . hasn't lost the glow after all these years of ministry"(Gary W. Demarest, *The Communicator's Commentary*, vol. 9.)

It is unknown if the doxology in verse 17 was directed at Jesus or the Father, but it is not at all inconsistent with what Paul has already said about Jesus. Your group should find and discuss more than a dozen phrases that describe Jesus in this text.

Question 3. Paul uses a variety of adjectives and nouns to describe himself both before and after his conversion. Be sure that the group picks up the indirect references as well, especially "example" in verse 16 and "sinner" in verse 15.

Question 4. Paul places the emphasis for his conversion clearly on the work and initiative of Christ Jesus: Jesus strengthened, judged, and appointed (v. 12), gave mercy, grace, faith, and love (vv. 13-14), saved (v. 15), and made Paul an example (v. 16). Because of all this, Paul includes a doxology in verse 17. Notice also that all of this work had a very specific purpose: to enable Paul to have a ministry in Jesus' name. For a narrative account of Paul's conversion, see Acts 9.

Question 5. This is a difficult phrase, because, as Fee puts it, "this sounds contradictory, as though he received mercy because he had it coming" (p. 51). It is clear, however, from the rest of the paragraph that Paul in no way thought that he did not need the grace offered by Jesus. Demarest suggests that the phrase is meant as a corrective to the way that testimonies of someone's conversion are often given: "Having described his past behavior, I hear him saying that there was nothing chic or glamorous about what he had done. As a matter of fact, it was grounded in his unbelief and thus utterly stupid" (p. 161).

Question 6. Few people have had a conversion experience as intense and life-changing as Paul's (see Acts 9:1-22). Most Christians, however, will find many points of contact with what Paul expresses in this passage. Use this question to allow each person to tell a bit of personal faith history. Be careful that anyone who is not yet a Christian also feels comfortable to express where he or she is in relation to Paul's experience.

Question 8. Both Paul and Timothy had been strengthened by God in various ways. Verse 18 seems to refer to Timothy's commissioning or ordination, which likely would have included prophetic utterances. Concerning New Testament prophecies, Demarest says, "We must not think of prophecy here primarily as a prediction . . . prophecy was more commonly an exhortation or an encouragement" (p. 164). Insofar as God calls each of us to minister in His name, we also need to be strengthened. This may often come through words of encouragement from others in the body of Christ.

If you need an extra question at this point ask: *In what ways do you need to be strengthened by Christ in order to do His will?*

Question 10. The idea of Paul turning members of the body of Christ over to Satan may seem like a strange idea. The meaning here is not really clear. It probably meant that Hymenaeus and Alexander were excluded from the church. According to Robert G. Gromacki, "Such a deliverance (to Satan) involves neither a consignment to Hades or the lake of fire nor a loss of salvation. Outside the church is the sphere of satanic dominion. . . . It is in that realm that Paul wanted to see the two adversaries chastised" (p. 45).

Whatever the phrase meant, "the most important thing to note is that the delivering to Satan was redemptive in its intent. Though some separation from active fellowship in the life of the church seems to be implied, there is still the hope that these men will be restored as they "learn not to blaspheme" (Demarest, p. 166).

Question 11. This may be a tricky question in some groups. Our society tends to communicate to people that their beliefs and actions are their own private matters. Many Christians would deny that a church has any right at all to "discipline" members. The other side of the issue is churches who have abused the biblical call of mutual accountability. "When church discipline becomes harsh and punitive, losing its goal of reconciliation and restoration, it can have devastating results" (Demarest, p. 166). Some members of the group may have had experiences with people in churches who were judgmental and did not have reconciliation as a goal.

Yet this passage implies a form of exclusion for specific offenses and for specific purpose. Help people in your group to build on this example in an attempt to construct reasonable principles of discipline for their own setting.

Study Three
Politically Correct?
1 Timothy 2:1-15

Purpose: To explore various controversies in the church in Paul's day and our own.

Question 1. You may notice that there are more opening questions than usual for this study. This is intentional, to insure that everyone has a chance to get settled and participate before jumping into a potentially difficult study. As a leader, be sure that you take enough time to get everyone warmed up, but also be careful to not take too much time, as the study itself could be lengthy.

Question 2. When answering the second part of the question, encourage group members to focus on the issue of women in leadership positions, and to avoid dwelling on the specific person in the position.

Questions 3–4. Before the passage is read, it may be a good idea to ask the group to imagine that Paul is speaking to them. This will help people to pay attention to their own responses. Different group members are likely to have considerably different responses to the passage. Some people may notice a verse from the first half, and be encouraged. Others may pick up on a verse from the second half and be put off. (Try not to have all of the discussion emphasis on a single section of the text.) The important things for the group leader to remember are that everyone should have a chance to give honest reactions, and that this is only the first question in the study.

Question 5. Paul gives two reasons to pray for everyone: first, "that we may lead a quiet and peaceable life . . . " and second, for the salvation of all as desired by God. The second is easily applicable to our situation, but the first purpose may be a bit foreign to people who live in a politically stable environment. (We may take that too much for granted, or focus too much on our own setting.) But the possibility of leading a quiet and peaceable life was an important issue to the early church, which resided in a country of emperor-worship. Roman authorities were lenient to a degree to monotheistic religions. Still, praying for "kings and all who are in high positions" (v. 2) showed Christians as good citizens of the society in which they lived (*Bible Background Commentary*), and gave prayer to the hope that they would be "allowed to practice their religion without fear of disturbance and to lead the morally serious life appropriate to it" (Kelly, p. 61).

If you want a follow-up question, consider: *If you were to place these instructions for prayer in your own setting, for whom would you pray — and how?*

Question 6. These verses contain several important points of doctrine. They also give some of the most clear statements found in Scripture about God's desire for everyone to experience salvation. In verse 4 this is stated explicitly. Then, verses 5-6 are part of an early creed witnessing to the saving work of Christ. Finally, in verse 7 Paul notes his call to be a teacher of the Gentiles, which was acted out evidence that God wants all people-groups to hear about Jesus.

Paul's reason for emphasizing God's desire for universal salvation is probably a response to the false teachers mentioned in chapter 1, who may have been teaching that only certain people (Jews, perhaps) were able to receive salvation (Fee, pp. 66–67).

These verses can also be seen as a strong call to evangelism and mission. If God desires all to be saved, and has at great cost provided the means, we Christians should be actively reaching out to people, both personally and as churches. For a powerful and compelling application of the meaning of these verses, see pages 169–175 of Demarest's commentary. God's love for all people means that we too must love all people without distinction.

Question 8. Evidently there were several seemingly unrelated things happening in the church. There were evidently men who did not pray or did not pray properly, arguments among the men, women who were dressed inappropriately, and women who were teaching/speaking in ways that Paul disapproved of. These were seen by Paul as distractions from proper worship and Christian living.

Each of these problems may have related to the teachers of false doctrine with which Paul opened his letter. Were these troublesome teachers uninformed women?

Question 9. Paul would no doubt find much of what we do in a worship service to be strange. But he would likely be most concerned about anything in worship that takes our focus away from

God and the work of Christ. Some concrete things—which may seem minor—that commonly happen in church: choir members who whisper throughout the service; musical solos that focus attention on the performer, and not on the content; people, both men and women, who make the worship service a fashion show; speakers who push their own divisive agendas.

Question 10. These four verses represent one of the hottest debates within American Christianity. The question of applying them to our situations is tricky because so many people feel strongly about the issues of women in ministry and authority. At the same time, few people would deny that these verses have something to say to the church today.

In general, most people who interpret this passage fall into one of two categories: (1) those who read Paul's words as universal commands for all Christians in all places, and (2) those who attempt to understand why Paul wrote these instructions to Timothy as he worked in the particular church at Ephesus.

Representative of the first group is Gromacki who writes "she (a woman) cannot have the formal position as a permanent, authoritative teacher in the church. . . . A woman also could not have an authoritative position over men in the church. She could not issue pronouncements of doctrine and practice that would have to be obeyed by men . . . even delegated authority, authorized by a congregational vote, would violate the principal of spiritual headship." For those who agree with Gromacki, what the apostle said to Timothy is essentially what God says to the church today.

Summarizing the interpretations of the second group is more difficult. Most, however, would follow three guidelines given by Demarest: (1) *We must read the passage in the light of all other Scripture.* There are numerous passages, especially in the New Testament, that include women in positions of leadership. Some of these are passages written by Paul himself, for example in the 16th chapter of Romans. (2) *We must distinguish between passages that describe events or practices at the time, and those that clearly teach principles designed for universal and timeless application.* The question for this passage, then, is: Did Paul write these instructions specifically for the church at Ephesus, in order to correct their specific problems? One common interpretation of the passage is to see that Paul was writing to a church where false teachers had led some of the congregation astray, particularly some women (1 Timothy 5:13, 2 Timothy 3:6). Because it was evidently women who were being deceived, Paul did not want these particular women to have authority or to teach. In this light, Paul's discussion in verses 13-14 makes perfect sense, since the Creation story shows Eve being deceived and leading Adam (who appeared to follow quite willingly) in the same direction.

(3) *We must read the passage within its cultural, social and historical setting.* Again, it is probable that Paul's argument is shaped by the setting to which he writes. According to Barclay "It (this passage) was written against a Jewish background . . . officially the position of a woman was very low. In Jewish law she was not a person but a thing . . . she was forbidden to learn the law." In short, a woman in Jewish society, out of which the early church grew, would very probably not be qualified to teach.

Questions may also come up regarding verse 15. This verse is quite difficult to interpret. Gordon Fee suggests the following:

> More likely what Paul intends is that woman's salvation, from the transgressions brought about by similar deception and ultimately for eternal life, is to be found in her being a model, godly woman, known for her good works (v. 10; cf. 5:11). And her good deeds, according to 5:11 and 14, include marriage, bearing children (the verb form of this noun), and keeping a good home. The reason for his saying that she *will be saved* is that it follows directly out of his having said "the woman came to be in transgression." But Paul could never leave the matter there, as though salvation were attained by this "good deed," so he immediately qualifies, 'provided of course that she is already a truly Christian woman," that is, a woman who *continues in faith, love, and holiness* (pp. 75–76).

For a more complete survey of possible meanings of this text, See Fee pages 75–76 or the *New International Version Study Bible.*

Study Four
Beyond Reproach
1 Timothy 3:1-13

Purpose: To explore the needs and requirements of church leaders

Question 1. Responses to this question may vary from the mundane and reasonable to the bizarre and unreasonable. Some examples might be: the pastor's wife should play the piano, teach Sunday School, direct the choir, and not work except as a public school teacher; pastor's children should know more about the Bible and talk less than anyone else's children; the pastor should always be available in an emergency—even when on vacation; the pastor should always be the last person to leave after a church function, preferably with the rest of the family.

Question 3. Watch to see that everyone gets a chance to contribute an answer. It may be a temptation for one or two people to just list off all the qualities of bishops, for example, without pausing to let anyone else talk. Be sure that your group points out both actions and restraints on each of the three sets of leaders.

A question may arise about the women mentioned in verse 11. It is not exactly clear who they are, since the Greek word used can be translated either "woman" or "wife." The context, however, would seem to imply some specific women, not just a pronouncement about women in general. The NRSV uses "women" precisely because it is uncertain if the women in question were wives of deacons, or actually in leadership roles themselves.

According to Gordon Fee, "In favor of 'wives' is that the deacons are addressed on either side of this verse. It is also argued that one might have expected more detail if a third category were envisioned. In favor of 'deaconesses' is the structure of the sentence itself, which is the exact equivalent of verse 8, both of which are dependent on the verb 'must' in verse 2 (thus implying three categories). It is further argued that had the wives of deacons been in view, Paul might have been expected to say 'their wives' (as the NIV does without any warrant whatsoever). Since there was no word in Greek for 'deaconess' . . . it is likely that 'women here would have been understood to mean women who served the church in some capacity' " (p. 88).

Questions 4–5. Be prepared for a variety of answers. Some group members may have had bad experiences with church leaders in the past, or even in the present. The public has an increasingly negative view of church leadership because of the recent publicity given to fallen church leaders. Encourage your group to give specific examples of these qualities and expectations played out by today's spiritual leaders.

Question 6. This question may seem a bit circular at first. But the way we look at the phrase "above reproach" can be very important. A parallel idea can be seen in the choosing of school crossing guards. When a teacher chooses someone to be a crossing guard, does the teacher look for someone who is already mature and responsible, or is there an assumption that the responsibilities of doing the job will bring out the best in a grade-school boy or girl, or is there a mixture of the two ideas?

Question 7. Many commentators have noted that this list does not contain a great deal of specifically Christian content. In fact, virtue lists such as this one were fairly common in the New Testament period. This may point to the need for church leaders to be well-thought-of by unbelievers, as specifically noted in verse 7.

The exception to this observation is that the bishop must be "married only once." The phrase "married only once," (literally, "the husband of one wife" in the Greek) is quite ambiguous. According to Fee, there are at least four reasonable ways to understand the phrase. The first is that Paul expected that bishops (and later deacons) should be married, and not single. (Of course Paul, and evidently Timothy, were not married.) Second, it could be seen as a prohibition of polygamy; however, that was evidently not a common practice in Paul's time. Third, it could be a prohibition against remarriage, after either death of a spouse or divorce. Finally, it could merely be a requirement of fidelity within an existing marriage. This might also assume much of the first three interpretations, but would be seen as a reaction to the teachings of the false teachers in 4:3. If we accept the fourth interpretation, the marital status is not the primary point, but rather the value of exemplary marriage (pp. 80–81).

Question 8. It may be that some group members would rather not talk specifically about a "church." But most people can talk about an experience in some sort of "faith community." Some other option might include a college ministry group, youth groups while growing up, or even an especially significant small group.

Question 9. When answering the first question, keep in mind that some group members may have been hurt personally by a church leader who "fell." It may be important for that person to talk at some length. Also be aware that the effects of a church leader's mistakes take place in both personal and public ways.

The second question may elicit responses that are theoretical as well as practical and specific, personal as well as public. If the discussion is particularly good, a follow-up question would be: "What are some ways that we can protect ourselves or our leaders from spiritual attacks?"

Question 10. It may be interesting to note that "double-tongued" is translated "indulging in double-talk" in the *New English Bible* and "be sincere" in the *New International Version* and *Good News Bible*. The Greek word literally means "having two tongues." The implication is that one tongue would say one thing to one person and the other something else to another person.

Question 11. It may be helpful at this point to insert a bit of history, in order to understand the context of Paul's words. The city of Ephesus had been an important port, and was still the pagan religious center of the area. Syncretism (the mixing of religions) was prominent, and fertility cults were common. In this context, Paul calls for the church leaders to remain separate from these other religions and hold fast to a faith that was still minor and new. This is the situation in which North American Christians increasingly find themselves. In a society which searches for a combination of religious experiences, it can be harder and harder for Christians to hold on to the "exclusivist" aspects of their faith. Besides the text itself describes the Christian faith as a "mystery." In a context of opposition, it is hard to hold to a faith that is, to some extent, mysterious and therefore defies full explanation.

With this in mind, you can encourage discussion by asking questions such as: *When do you feel pressure to not talk to others about Christ? What topics do you feel are not acceptable with your non-Christian friends? How can you be true to your faith in a context where all religions are considered equal? What do you find hard to explain about the Christian faith?* After this discussion, a good follow-up question might be: *How can other believers help you hold fast to the Christian faith?*

Question 12. In a time when the public mistakes of prominent Christian leaders has severely damaged the reputation of our churches, it is increasingly important that church leaders at all levels be chosen carefully. Also, the various forms of abuse (physical, sexual, emotional, and spiritual) that have lately been publicized should compel Christians to seriously examine the effects that authority can have when it is not properly handled.

Some Christian groups have called for extensive background checks on everyone from Sunday School teachers to pastors—including running an inquiry with law enforcement agencies and scrutinizing references. Others require a period of spiritual examination and training before a person takes a leadership position. Let your group discuss these and other ways that we can obey this passage and thereby safeguard the reputation of Christ's church.

Question 14. If it is appropriate, you might ask a follow-up question something like: *In what ways can a group like this help you to be above reproach?*

Study Five
True Religion
1 Timothy 3:14–4:5

Purpose: To understand how to discern between what is beneficial and what is harmful to our faith.

Question 4. Group members may pick up several different ways of answering this question. One less than obvious difference is that in the first part the emphasis is on Christ—and what has happened to Him; in the second part the false teachers seem to emphasize what people are to do—or not do. Paul also shows the battle lines to be spiritual, by connecting the false teachers with demons.

Question 5. According to these two verses, Paul is concerned that a delay in his trip to Ephesus might prove too costly to the church, a church that needs to know now how "to behave in the household of God." Paul is thinking again of the false teachers and how Timothy can counter their wrong teachings—as he said in the first chapter. This time, however, Paul emphasizes the importance of actions in response to the false teachers.

Question 6. If someone in your group knows how to do liturgical chant, ask him or her to sing the lines several times, to help the group focus on the work of Christ. In using the hymn found in verse 16, Paul was probably quoting lines that Timothy was already familiar with, and perhaps was using in the worship at Ephesus. Scholars are not certain exactly what the formation of the hymn means. The *Bible Background Commentary* notes that "if 'taken up in glory' refers to Jesus' return (cf. Daniel 7:13-14) rather than to His ascension, then the lines are in chronological order."

If there is confusion about the meaning of lines two or three, it might be helpful to know that some translations read "vindicated by the (Holy) Spirit" for line two. It is likely that the second line refers to the Resurrection, where the judgment of the human authorities was overturned by God the Father. "Was seen by angels" could refer to the ascension, or to events in the life of Christ (for example, Matthew 4:11). Also, "Gentiles" in line 4 can also be translated "nations." Either way, it was surely meant to communicate the universal scope of the preaching of Christ.

As your group absorbs this hymn, encourage responses that reflect not only understanding but also personal reactions of worship and action.

Question 7. Paul uses strong imagery and language to condemn his opponents. He seems to set up three groups: the "deceitful spirits" whose teachings are demonic; the "liars" who seem to be the false teachers; and those who "renounce the faith," probably former members of the "household of God" mentioned in 3:15. Notice that Paul refers to the false teachers as hypocritical liars, emphasizing that they not only teach what is false, but are evidently not following through on what they teach, which invalidates any supposed value of their teachings. The teachers have evidently been "branded" by the deceitful spirits as their own. Paul must have assumed that the Ephesian church would recognize this "brand" although we can't really know what it would have been.

The teachings of the opponents refuted in this section have to do with a false asceticism. In other letters Paul allows, even encourages, a righteous asceticism (especially in his first letter to the Corinthians). But the false teachers of Ephesus seem to have tied asceticism to some sort of elitist salvation.

Question 8. In responding to the false asceticism, Paul focuses on the fact that what God has created is good—if it is taken and used by those "who believe and know the truth." One small expression of this attitude of thanksgiving is a simple thank-you prayer at the table. The early church likely carried on the Jewish table blessings, which were similar to the "grace" often said today before meals: "Jewish people always praised God before their meal; the normal blessing included praise for the God who 'created' the fruit of the vine" *(Bible Background Commentary)*.

Question 10. Try to keep the group focused on this particular passage and what we can learn from it. Some group members may refer to other biblical passages—especially some of Paul's other writings. If possible, exhaust the passage at hand first, then refer to other sources.

Study Six
Godly Training
1 Timothy 4:6-16

Purpose: To explore our need for spiritual training and ways we can use our gifts.

Question 2. This passage is the place in the letter where Paul gives most of the advice meant for Timothy himself. It is in contrast to most of the letter, which is meant for the whole church. This passage contains numerous imperative verbs, stressing the seriousness of what Paul had to tell Timothy. Your group should note and discuss more than a dozen commands in the text.

Question 5. The myths and old wives' tales are probably references to the teachings of Paul's opponents, and were likely meant to bring to mind the false asceticism condemned earlier in the chapter. Although we do not know the content of these teachings, we do know that Paul opposed them not only for their content, but also for the distractions they caused. Your group can find potential answers in 1 Timothy 1:3-7, 19-20; 4:1-3.

As for current myths and old wives' tales, your group should mention several that threaten to dilute the truth. The return to pagan stories and worship forms popular in this "New Age" may provide some examples. Other myths and tales grow out of the traditional church. Examples might include: God wants you to be healthy and wealthy. Black people descended from Ham and therefore are cursed by God. If something good happens to you, you "must be living right."

Question 6. According to Fee, "The word *eusebeia* ('true godliness') is used throughout 1 Timothy to express genuine Christian faith — the truth and its visible expression" (p. 104). So godliness has two aspects: a set of beliefs (such as those described in 2:5-6 and 3:16), and a desired set of actions. For Paul, both were important, especially in a culture hostile to Christianity, where believers had to continually prove their integrity. The same is often true for Christians today, who must show that their faith leads them to act differently from the rest of society.

Question 7. Help your group to study the variety of explanations for the hard work of training expressed throughout verses 7-11. Then continue the discussion on a more personal level. The word Paul uses for "train yourself" brings to mind a metaphor which was understood in Paul's time much the same as it is today. An athlete must train in a way that "stresses constant, strenuous activity that will increase strength and ability" (Gromacki, p. 117). Spiritual training is similar. It involves study of the truth, especially as found in Scripture, as well as "training" ourselves to obey the truth and to act in ways that bring glory to God, and not to ourselves. Your group should notice that verse 11 emphasizes the importance of these concepts — and returns to the theme of the book when Paul says, "These are the things you must insist on and teach."

Question 8. Your group should find and discuss about a dozen ways, in verses 12-16, that would help a person to lead by example. In addition, this passage points out three tools Timothy had to work with. First, he could teach by using himself as an example. This would be especially effective, because of his connection to the Apostle Paul, who was certainly not afraid to use himself as an example of one who endeavored to follow Jesus. (See 1 Timothy 1:16, Philippians 3:17) Second, Paul tells Timothy to use Scripture. Finally, he is to "not neglect the gift" that is in him. This gift may well have been the "spiritual gift" of teaching. Whichever gift it was, Paul expected it to help Timothy to be effective in combatting the false teachers, and thus preserve the truth of the Gospel. For more about Timothy's gift, see the note for question 8 of study 2.

Question 9. Help your group to examine the text again, this time looking for the relationship between leading by teaching and leading by example. Paul interweaves teaching and example throughout this section — suggesting that, in the best Christian leadership, they are intertwined in practice as well.

Question 10. Encourage each person to respond in some way to these suggestions for good leadership. People can look at their leadership opportunities at work, at church, in the home, in their friendships, in the community. Guide the discussion toward ways in each setting that people can lead by their example of honoring and obeying God in the small affairs of life. For instance, a pastor may (at times) teach more by washing dishes in the church kitchen than by standing in the pulpit.

Questions 11–12. Use this opportunity to close your study by expressing thanks for other Christians who have encouraged us to serve God with all that we are. Then affirm each other by acknowledging the strengths God has given and encourage the use of these strengths in His work.

Study Seven
Honoring the Needy
1 Timothy 5:1-16

Purpose: To explore how we can offer both help and honor to the needy.

Question 1. It will be important that as many group members as possible respond to this question so that they can identify with the widows spoken of in the passage. Besides the examples mentioned in the question, we may also feel isolated when someone close to us has died, when we are lost, or when we are starting a new job or college class. Encourage each person to describe some personal experience of feeling isolated.

Question 2. Several different relationships are mentioned in verses 1-2. Take appropriate note of these, then move to the rest of the passage. After verse 2, the relationships center around the different groups of widows. Be sure that the group notices the relationship between the widows and the whole church. There is also an implicit relationship between the widows and Jesus, although for some of the widows, this relationship seems to be not as important.

Question 3. Once again, make sure the group notices the responsibilities in the relationship between the church and the "real widows," especially that there are responsibilities for both the widows and the church. Don't forget to draw attention to the responsibilities toward the ordinary fellow-believers described in verses 1 and 2.

Question 5. Paul seems to be concerned that those who have responsibilities toward their parents are encouraged to follow through. There is probably also a sense of making sure that the church is able to give priority to those most in need. Encourage group members to understand Paul's teachings here—but also to discuss its implications on their own families.

Question 7. Paul has at least two concerns about the younger widows. The first is that they will want to remarry. Barclay notes "It is not that younger widows are condemned for marrying again. What is condemned is this. A young husband dies; and the widow . . . decides to remain a widow all her life and dedicate her life to the Church; but later she changes her mind and remarries. That woman is regarded as having taken Christ as bridegroom" (p. 114). That Paul is not condemning marriage in general is obvious from verse 14. There he tells Timothy that young widows (and widowers?) ought to marry and raise families.

The second concern is that the younger widows had too much time on their hands, and had become victims of the false teachers, whose erroneous teachings they were now distributing. According to Fee, "The translation 'gossips' *(phlyaroi)* is quite misleading, suggesting on the basis of 'going from house to house' that they are involved in 'idle talk about the affairs of others.' The Greek word, however, means 'to talk nonsense' or foolishness, and is used most often in contexts of speaking something foolish or absurd in comparison to truth" (p. 122). This may in fact be the basis for Paul's comments about women in authority or teaching positions in 2:12-15. It seems likely that both concerns expressed above rose out of the situation in Ephesus, where damage was already in progress.

People who are new to this passage may feel that Paul's statements here about young widows are unduly harsh — even prejudiced against women. It will help to focus on the reasons for his concern as explained in verses 14-15.

Question 8. It is not clear from the text if the list Paul refers to implies that there is some sort of organized "order of widows," or if it is just an ad hoc arrangement, which sprang up in response to a need. Hanson and Kelly believe that widows on the list actually took a vow to chastity, which is referred to later in verse 12. But there is no evidence from the text to suggest so. Fee suggests that, "he (Paul) is not so much setting up duties in verse 10 . . . as he is arguing that she must *already* (probably before as well as after her husband's death) be *well known for her good deeds*"(p. 119).

Question 10. Use what you have studied in this text to help the group discern "real" need — then outline practical ways the church can serve in those situations. Paul was not trying to talk the church out of a job; he was helping it focus on root problems and solutions that granted protection and dignity. We should do the same.

Study Eight
A Double Honor
1 Timothy 5:17–6:2a

Question 3. It will probably be helpful to have extra paper available for this question. If the group is to do the exercise together, then perhaps a piece of poster board, or something similar, would be appropriate. If the group resists being visually creative, encourage them to orally describe the flow of the passage.

Question 4. Several different answers are possible. Most scholars assume that part of the double honor was financial compensation. Karris believes that this meant a "double honorarium" (p. 95). Fee, however, argues that "it means 'twofold honor,' the honor and respect due those in such positions as well as remuneration" (p. 129). Fee's conclusion makes the most sense, but the important point is that Paul desires that Timothy make sure that the church leaders are cared for, much as the widows were to be cared for.

Some churches today have two kinds of elders. Teaching elders (pastors) are usually paid. But the church also has ruling elders who are responsible for the spiritual oversight of the church. These people serve as volunteers, but they also are to receive "honor" even though that honor is not monetary.

Question 5. Paul supports his command by referring to an Old Testament passage (Deuteronomy 25:4) and a saying of Jesus (Luke 10:7). Both stress that the leaders are to be rewarded for what they have done, and not as some fringe benefit of a position.

The mental picture created by the text graphically portrays what a church is *not* to do. We see a tethered ox walking round and round a millstone grinding out grain—his own mouth muzzled against eating. How tragic that many pastors are the least served people of the congregation. If it seems appropriate, ask group members to discuss what types of church positions they think should be paid and why.

Questions 6–7. There seems to be two opposite dangers here.

Paul is first of all concerned, as he has been throughout the book, about the activities of false teachers. Because of the trouble they are stirring up, it is necessary to outline actions needed to stop their false teachings. Those who *persist* in sin must be exposed publicly. Notice the connection to Matthew 18:15-20.

The second danger is probably more hypothetical. Whenever there is legitimate curtailing of sin, there is the possibility that honest, sincere people will become the targets of malicious accusations. Paul uses a traditional rule to insure that innocent elders are not falsely accused. (See Deuteronomy 19:15.)

Paul is probably especially concerned about the elders for two reasons. Their visibility within the faith community made it easy for them to cause others to follow in their erroneous footsteps. Also, their visibility among non-believers would have communicated all the wrong messages to a society which needed to hear the true Gospel. Both concerns seem very relevant for today's situation.

Question 8. Your group may remember ill-founded allegations against such well-known leaders as Madeline L'Engle, Karen Mains, Tony Campolo, and Billy Graham. They may also remember other leaders who should have been confronted by the Christian community long before the secular legal system brought them to justice. Encourage discussion of our personal responsibility in these kinds of situations.

Question 9. This question may require some sensitivity. In some groups this may be an opportunity to be very specific, especially if the trust level is high, and group members respect confidentiality. In other groups, especially those that function within a church, it may be wiser to stick to general answers, and not name individuals. In either case, the emphasis of the dialogue should be on how to follow Paul's words better, and not an opportunity to gossip or slander those not present.

Question 10. The identity of those who receive the laying on of hands is unclear in this passage. Some commentators, such as Hanson (p. 103), believe this is a reference to reinstating penitent sinners into the church. Some, such as Fee (p. 131), believe that it refers to the ordaining of elders. Either way, Paul seems to say that those who lay hands on others, do so at the risk of some responsibility for any sins later committed.

Question 11. This is a passage which has troubled many people, both because of its content and its placement. As for placement, we can see it as a jotted personal note in the middle of instructions for the whole church. Regarding content, Paul says, "No longer drink . . ." so Timothy is evidently abstaining from wine, perhaps because of pressure from those who follow the asceticism of the false teachers (see 4:1-5). Paul seems to say that Timothy's health is more important than offending the moral sensibilities of those who would diminish the importance of our physical existence. Commentators seem to agree, however, that this passage should not be read as a license to drink alcohol in excess. Elsewhere, Paul speaks strongly against drunkenness (as in Ephesians 5:18), and he has already told Timothy in 3:3 that bishops are not to be drunkards. Like the passages on women, this verse is best understood in its social context.

Question 13. This is another difficult question, because Paul completely avoids the horrors of slavery, and actually asks the slaves to go out of their way to please their masters. Kelly notes that Paul's comments here are in line with Jesus' attitude (p. 131), and it is consistent with Paul's call to serve each other in other letters (Philippians 2).

Study Nine
The Good Fight
1 Timothy 6:2b-16

Purpose: To find encouragement to continue in our faith, even when we are faced with adversity.

Question 2. Paul gives a list in verse 11, and verses 13-15 give a glimpse of what is *ultimately* important. Just as interesting, though, is what Paul considers unimportant, as seen in verses 4-5 and 9-10. Rather than just taking note of the verses, encourage your group to point out and discuss significant issues in each section. They may notice significant contrasts with today's secular value system. They may also notice (as Paul did) that some of that value system has infiltrated the church.

Question 3. Paul poses at least two tests in this verse. The first is the "duties" he has described beginning with the opening words of chapter 5. The second are the "sound words of our Lord Jesus Christ," thus assuming a common knowledge of Christ's teachings probably recorded in early versions of the Gospels. Paul is arguing here that those who do not agree with these teachings are everything listed in verses 4-5. In fact, Fee says Paul's emphasis is "that the false teachers have abandoned the truth of the Gospel, which comes from our Lord Jesus Christ Himself, who is the ultimate origin of the faith or 'godliness' Paul proclaimed (p. 141)."

Question 5. Your group should notice that ultimately Paul seems to stress that our contentment depends primarily on our state of mind, that our view is eternal—on what we can (and cannot) take out of this world. This is in direct contrast to our advertising culture, which stresses that it is the things we buy and achieve that will bring us happiness.

Question 6. Your group may benefit from a few minutes of silence for thoughtful self-evaluation before venturing into this question. Encourage each person, who is willing, to respond to this question.

Question 9. In this passage Paul makes the good fight sound like a great battle of will, in which Timothy must persevere over his own timidity. Of course, if you use these verses to measure the actions of Jesus' disciples after his arrest, they would have all flunked. Encourage group members to use these verses to measure their own struggles to continue in faith.

Question 11. Timothy may still have been a little intimidated by the false teachers, who were probably older than he, and probably sounded very wise. A reminder of who is ultimately in control and who really has all the answers would no doubt bolster Timothy's resolve. After the group has discussed Timothy's needs, help people to focus on themselves and their own responses to Almighty God, as He is praised in this wonderful doxology.

Study Ten
Using Our Riches
1 Timothy 6:17-21

Purpose: To explore the various ways God gives to us, and how we put what God gives us to good use.

Question 1. Depending on the makeup of your group, this could turn into a lively discussion. After all, Jesus had some strong, even harsh things to say about rich people. Use the question to explore the diversity of attitudes within your group, even diversity within the same person over a period of time.

Question 3. Notice that the command to the rich is similar to the description of the real widow in 1 Timothy 5:5. Before God, they are not only equal, but should have the same frame of mind.

Question 4. Your group may at first focus on haughtiness about monetary wealth. (The passage does.) But the same principles apply to all that God has given us. Encourage people to consider situations where they feel intellectually superior, or educationally advanced, or spiritually "mature." These are all gifts from God, and they can all tempt us toward haughtiness.

Question 5. Your group should discuss the relationship between verses 18 and 19.

Questions 6–7. Christians who are rich have an obvious opportunity to create change. As North Americans, most of us are rich by the standards of the rest of the world. As wealthy citizens of the world, we tend to give priority to things that are not necessities. What would happen, for example, if every Christian in your city stopped drinking carbonated beverages, and gave the money saved to support homes for abused children, or food pantries? Use questions 6 and 7 to help your group examine their own lives.

Question 10. Paul just can't seem to go very long without mentioning his opponents. This parting shot gives one last warning to Timothy, and the congregation, to stay away from false teachers.

For Further Reading

Aharoni, Yohanan, and Michael Avi-Yonah, eds. *The MacMillan Bible Atlas*. Revised Edition, New York and London: Collier MacMillan Publishers, 1977.

Barclay, William. *The Letters to Timothy, Titus and Philemon*. The Daily Study Bible Series. Philadelphia: The Westminster Press, 1975.

Clouse, Robert and Bonnidell Clouse, eds. *Women in Ministry: Four Views*. Downers Grove, Ill.: InterVarsity Press, 1989.

Demarest, Gary W. *1, 2 Thessalonians, 1, 2 Timothy, Titus*. The Communicator's Commentary. Vol. 9. Waco, Texas: Word, 1978.

Dibelius, Martin and Hans Conzelmann. *The Pastoral Epistles*. Hermeneia — A Critical and Historical Commentary of the Bible. Philadelphia: Fortress Press, 1972.

Douglas, J.D., F.F. Bruce, J.I. Packer, N. Hillyer, D. Guthrie, A.R. Millard, and D.J. Wiseman, eds. *New Bible Dictionary*. 2d ed. Leicester, England: Inter-Varsity Press, 1982.

Fee, Gordon. *1 and 2 Timothy, Titus*. New International Biblical Commentary. Vol. 13. Peabody, Mass.: Hendrickson, 1984, 1988.

Fee, Gordon D., and Douglas Stuart. *How to Read the Bible for All It's Worth*. Grand Rapids: Zondervan, 1981.

Ferguson, Sinclair B. and David F. Wright, eds. *New Dictionary of Theology*. Downers Grove, Ill. and Leicester, England: Inter-Varsity Press, 1988.

Finzel, Hans. *Observe Interpret Apply: How to Study the Bible Inductively*. Wheaton, Ill.: Victor Books, 1994.

Gorman, Julie A. *Community That is Christian: A Handbook for Small Groups*. Wheaton, Ill.: Victor Books, 1993.

About the Author

Scott Hotaling first got interested in Paul's letters to Timothy while working on his M. Div. degree at Northern Baptist Seminary. The letters' emphasis on sound teaching and the interworkings of a healthy church, along with Scott's great love for the Greek language, combined to inspire him to work with the biblical text for over a year. Creating a discussion guide is one way of passing on some of that excitement.

Scott grew up in Ottawa, Kansas, and then graduated from Sioux Falls College with a degree in Inter-Disciplinary Studies. Even in high school, he participated in small Bible study groups. Later he began to lead groups and continued to participate in them throughout college and beyond. Writing group discussion material became a natural next step.

His first experience with writing Bible study guides for publication had some astounding results. He and fellow-student Cindy Bunch (who is Bible Study Editor for InterVarsity Press), were working together on two guides for InterVarsity's "Created Male and Female Bible Studies." They must have ironed out most of their gender differences because, when they finished the books, they got married!

Scott and Cindy live in Wheaton, Illinois with their cocker spaniel, Sachi. When Scott is not writing Bible study guides, he works for Outreach Community Ministries as a recreation director with children in a low-income area. He also plays piano for his own pleasure and for his church.